Highway Accident Report

School Bus and Dump Truck Collision
Central Bridge, New York
October 21, 1999

NTSB/HAR-00/02
PB2000-916202
Notation 7302
Adopted November 14, 2000

National Transportation Safety Board
490 L'Enfant Plaza, S.W.
Washington, D.C. 20594

National Transportation Safety Board. 2000. *School Bus and Dump Truck Collision, Central Bridge, New York, October 21, 1999.* **Highway Accident Report NTSB/HAR-00/02. Washington, DC.**

Abstract: On October 21, 1999, about 10:30 a.m. near Central Bridge, New York, a school bus was transporting 44 students and 8 adults on a field trip. The bus was traveling north on State Route 30A as it approached the intersection with State Route 7. Concurrently, a dump truck, towing a utility trailer, was traveling west on State Route 7. As the bus approached the intersection, it failed to stop as required and was struck by the dump truck. Seven bus passengers sustained serious injuries; 28 bus passengers and the truckdriver received minor injuries. Thirteen bus passengers, the busdriver, and the truck passenger were uninjured.

The major safety issues discussed in this report are potential for passenger injuries as a result of the school bus emergency exit door design, the potential for passenger injuries as a result of school bus seat cushion bottoms that are removable or hinged, and the adequacy of commercial vehicle airbrake inspections.

As a result of this accident investigation, the Safety Board issued recommendations to the National Highway Traffic Safety Administration, the Federal Motor Carrier Safety Administration, the National Association of State Directors of Pupil Transportation Services, the Maintenance Council of the American Trucking Associations, and the Commercial Vehicle Safety Alliance. In addition, safety recommendations were reiterated to the National Highway Traffic Safety Administration.

Contents

Acronyms and Abbreviations

AmTran	American Transportation Corporation
CDL	commercial driver's license
CFR	*Code of Federal Regulations*
CVSA	Commercial Vehicle Safety Alliance
FMVSSs	*Federal Motor Vehicle Safety Standards*
I-88	Interstate 88
Kinnicutt	Kinnicutt Bus Company
MUTCD	*Manual on Uniform Traffic Control Devices*
MVF	MVF Construction Company
NASDPTS	National Association of State Directors of Pupil Transportation Services
NHTSA	National Highway Traffic Safety Administration
NYDMV	New York Department of Motor Vehicles
NYSDOT	New York State Department of Transportation
psi	pounds per square inch
SR-30A	State Route 30A
SR-7	State Route 7
TPV	tractor protection valve

Executive Summary

About 10:30 a.m. on October 21, 1999, in Schoharie County, New York, a Kinnicutt Bus Company school bus was transporting 44 students, 5 to 9 years old, and 8 adults on an Albany City School No. 18 field trip. The bus was traveling north on State Route 30A as it approached the intersection with State Route 7, which is about 1.5 miles east of Central Bridge, New York. Concurrently, an MVF Construction Company dump truck, towing a utility trailer, was traveling west on State Route 7. The dump truck was occupied by the driver and a passenger. As the bus approached the intersection, it failed to stop as required and was struck by the dump truck. Seven bus passengers sustained serious injuries; 28 bus passengers and the truckdriver received minor injuries. Thirteen bus passengers, the busdriver, and the truck passenger were uninjured.

The National Transportation Safety Board determines that the probable cause of this accident was the school bus driver's failure to stop for the stop sign due to his degraded performance or lapse of attention as a result of factors associated with aging or his medical condition or both.

The following major safety issues were identified in this accident:

- the potential for passenger injuries as a result of the school bus emergency exit door design,

- the potential for passenger injuries as a result of school bus seat cushion bottoms that are removable or hinged, and

- the adequacy of commercial vehicle airbrake inspections.

The medical fitness of commercial drivers and the medical examination for the commercial driver's license were also identified as safety issues; however, these issues will be analyzed in a forthcoming Safety Board special investigation report.

As a result of this accident investigation, the Safety Board makes recommendations to the National Highway Traffic Safety Administration, the Federal Motor Carrier Safety Administration, the National Association of State Directors of Pupil Transportation Services, the Maintenance Council of the American Trucking Associations, and the Commercial Vehicle Safety Alliance. In addition, safety recommendations are being reiterated to the National Highway Traffic Safety Administration.

Factual Information

Accident Narrative

About 7:20 a.m. on October 21, 1999, in Albany, New York, a 79-year-old school bus driver began transporting students to school on his regular morning route. He drove a 1997 American Transportation Corporation (AmTran) full-size school bus, owned and operated by the Kinnicutt Bus Company (Kinnicutt). About 8:50 a.m., after finishing his regular route, he drove to Albany City School No. 18 and loaded 44 children, 5 to 9 years old, and 8 adults (chaperons) for a scheduled field trip to the Pumpkin Patch in Central Bridge, New York, about 40 miles from the school.

The busdriver stated that he had never been to the Pumpkin Patch. No directions to the site had been provided by Kinnicutt for him to use. According to one chaperon, the busdriver said that he knew the general area to which he was going vaguely but not specifically. The chaperon said that the busdriver asked him for directions. The chaperon then went into the school and was able to obtain a map and directions from a teacher for the busdriver to use.

Each school bus passenger seat was equipped with three color-coded lap belts. These belts were attached to the seatframe at the juncture between the seatback and seat cushion bottom. According to the adult passengers, all of the children were restrained by a lap belt before the trip began.[1] The chaperons said that, to better supervise the children, the adults, except the one seated next to the emergency exit door, were unrestrained.

The bus departed the school about 9:20 a.m. The busdriver took the New York State Thruway west to exit 25A onto Interstate-88 (I-88) and then traveled west on I-88 toward exit 23, the intended exit. The chaperons stated that the busdriver seemed confused about the directions to the Pumpkin Patch and that he turned off at exit 24, the wrong exit. He ultimately stopped the bus on the exit 24 ramp. One chaperon reported that the driver appeared confused when he stopped on the ramp. She stated that she was concerned about where he positioned the bus on the ramp when he stopped; she feared that it would be struck by another vehicle. After the busdriver received directions from a chaperon, the driver returned to I-88 and continued traveling to exit 23, the correct exit.

The busdriver stated that at the top of the exit 23 ramp, he turned right onto State Route 30A (SR-30A) and started looking for State Route 7 (SR-7). About 10:30 a.m., the bus was traveling north on SR-30A between 15 and 25 mph[2] as it approached the intersection with SR-7. The intersection was about 1.5 miles east of Central Bridge. The north- and southbound traffic on SR-30A were controlled by an advance warning sign that

---

[1] Chaperons noted that some belts had to be unknotted or pulled from underneath or behind the seats before being used.

[2] Speed of bus based on vehicle dynamic simulation.

indicated a stop ahead, a stop sign, flashing red intersection control beacons,[3] and pavement markings that included the word "stop" and a stop bar.

At the same time, an MVF Construction Company (MVF) dump truck, towing a utility trailer, was traveling about 45 mph[4] west on SR-7. East- and westbound traffic on SR-7 at the intersection were controlled by flashing yellow intersection control beacons. The dump truck was occupied by its 52-year-old driver and a passenger.

As the school bus approached the intersection, according to the chaperons, several children on board saw the sign for the Pumpkin Patch that was beyond the intersection and yelled. These children may also have released their belt buckles. One child reportedly stood up in the seating compartment. The busdriver, who was looking for SR-7, told investigating police that he saw the posted stop sign, slowed, but did not stop the bus, which then entered the intersection where the dump truck struck it on the right side behind the rear axle. (See figure 1.)

Figure 1. Exterior crush damage of school bus.

---

[3] An intersection control beacon consists of one or more sections of a standard traffic signal head having flashing yellow or red indications in each face. It is used at intersections where traffic or physical conditions do not justify a conventional traffic signal but where high accident rates indicate a potential hazard.

[4] Speed of truck estimated by truckdriver.

The school bus, after rotating about 145 degrees clockwise, slid approximately 100 feet and came to rest facing south. The dump truck, after rotating about 150 degrees clockwise, struck three highway guide signs and a utility pole; it then came to rest facing northeast. (See figures 2 and 3.)

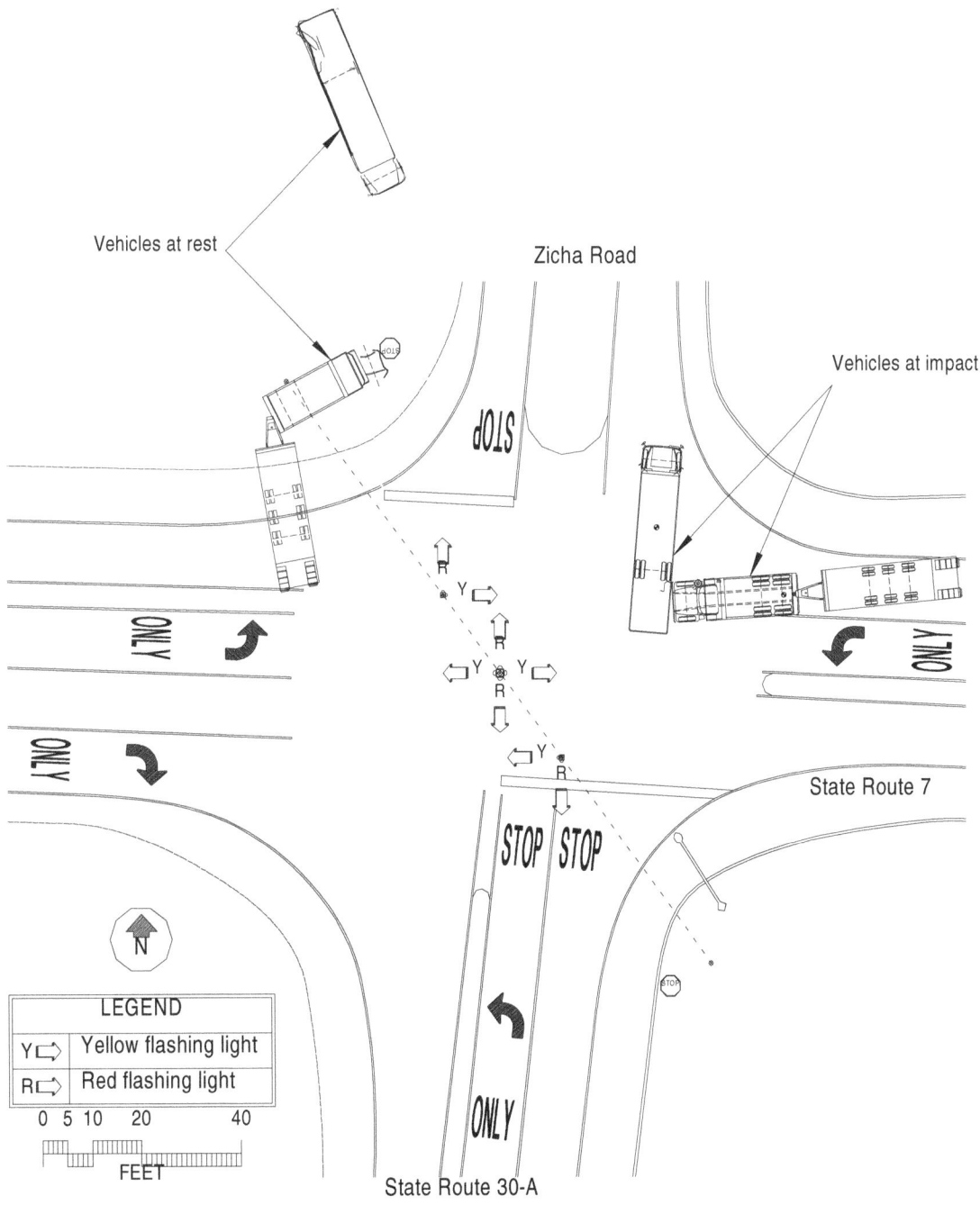

Figure 2. Diagram of vehicles at impact and final rest positions.

Figure 3. Final rest positions of vehicles.

During the postcrash interview with investigating police,[5] the school bus driver stated, "I was looking for route 7. As I approached the intersection in front of me, I saw a stop sign on the right side of the road. I was so concerned trying to find route 7 that I didn't stop. I only slowed down. I didn't stop before crossing route 7." The busdriver indicated that he never saw the approaching MVF truck. As he entered the intersection, he heard one of the chaperons shout, but he did not understand what was said. The MVF truck then struck the school bus.

The dump truckdriver said that he was familiar with the accident intersection.[6] In describing the accident, he stated that he was driving about 45 mph westbound on SR-7, approaching the intersection with SR-30A. He saw a flashing yellow control beacon at the intersection for his direction of travel. He noticed that the school bus was not slowing down for the stop at the intersection. He stated that he applied the truck brakes and attempted to steer to the left to avoid the collision. He did not remember any other vehicles being at the intersection before the accident.

---

[5] The school bus driver declined repeated Safety Board requests for an interview.

[6] The MVF office was 0.3 mile from the intersection.

Emergency Response

Immediately after the collision, the dump truckdriver contacted the local 911 dispatcher on his cellular telephone. The dispatcher contacted the Central Bridge Fire Department and Scho-Wright Ambulance Company, which were the emergency responders closest to the accident scene. At this time, the Schoharie County deputy fire coordinator and emergency medical services coordinator were monitoring their radios and responded to the accident. Mutual aid was requested; 12 emergency medical service ambulances and another fire department responded to the scene.

Chaperons reported that after the collision, they helped several children remove their lap belts to evacuate the bus. A chaperon told Safety Board investigators that all of the children with minor or no injuries were evacuated out of the front loading door of the bus. A passing school bus was flagged down, and these children were placed on that bus. They were then transferred to another bus, where they were evaluated by an emergency responder, and then taken to local hospitals for further examination.

A chaperon remained on the accident bus with three seriously injured passengers, two children and one adult. These passengers were evacuated out of the side emergency exit door on back boards and were transported to local hospitals by helicopter.

Injuries

Seven bus passengers sustained serious injuries;[7] 28 bus passengers and the truckdriver received minor injuries; and 13 bus passengers, the busdriver, and the truck passenger were uninjured. (See table 1.)[8]

Table 1. Injuries.

Injuries	Busdriver	Bus Passengers	Truck	Total
Fatal	0	0	0	0
Serious	0	7	0	7
Minor	0	28	1	29
None	1	13	1	15
Total	1	48	2	51

---

[7] Title 49 *Code of Federal Regulations* 830.2 defines a serious injury as an injury that requires hospitalization for more than 48 hours, commencing within 7 days from the date the injury was received; results in a fracture of any bone (except simple fractures of the fingers, toes, or nose); causes severe hemorrhages or nerve, muscle, or tendon damage; involves any internal organ; or involves second or third degree burns or any burns affecting more than 5 percent of the body surface.

Serious injuries included vertebra and skull fractures and internal injuries. Minor injuries included lacerations, abrasions, and neck strains. The most seriously injured passengers were seated in the area of impact. (See figure 4.)

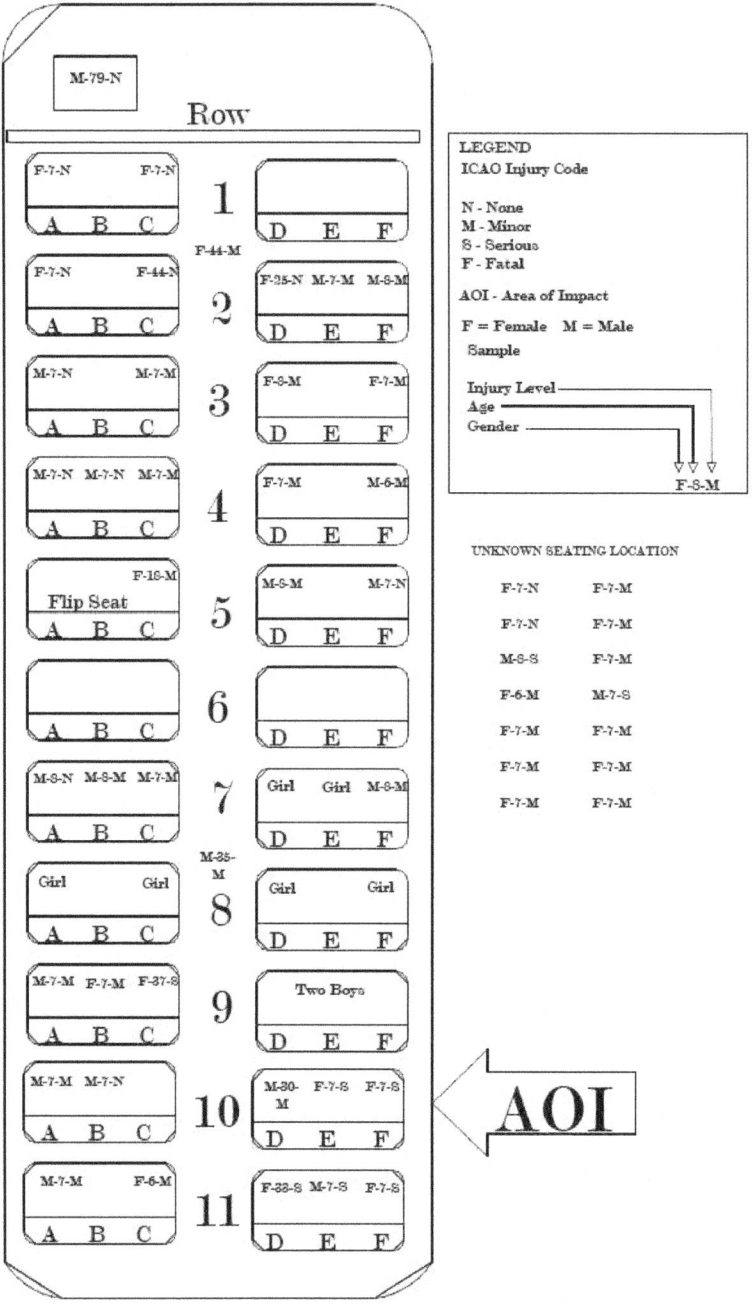

Figure 4. School bus seating and injury diagram.

---

[8] The medical records of four bus passengers were not obtained. Two passengers each were taken to two separate hospitals. Both hospitals refused to respond to the Safety Board's efforts, by subpoena and subsequent phone calls, to obtain medical records. The Safety Board chose not to pursue obtaining these records further. The information received on scene indicated that these passengers received minor injuries.

Driver Information

Busdriver

The school bus driver held a valid, class B, New York commercial driver's license (CDL) with passenger endorsement and corrective lens restriction.[9] The license was issued on February 20, 1992, and expires on March 31, 2003. The busdriver also possessed a current biennial[10] medical examiner's certificate that was issued on September 4, 1999. A review of his driving record revealed that he was involved in a property damage traffic accident in a school bus on October 20, 1997.[11] His record revealed no other traffic accidents, citations, or complaints about his driving. On December 6, 1999, the busdriver was convicted of "failing to stop at a stop sign" with respect to this accident.

Kinnicutt officials stated that the driver had been employed with the company since September 1, 1966. Before his employment with Kinnicutt, he was a local law enforcement officer. Company officials reported that he worked full-time, had been assigned his regular school route for 6 years, and was a conscientious driver. The busdriver's usual morning route began at 7:00 and ended at 8:30 a.m.; his usual afternoon route began at 3:00 and ended at 4:30 p.m. On the Monday and Tuesday before the accident, the busdriver drove to an apple orchard between 9:00 a.m. and 12:30 p.m., in addition to driving his usual route. On the Wednesday before the accident, he drove his usual routes and made no extra trips. Safety Board investigators were unable to obtain further details regarding his activities 72 hours before the accident.[12]

Since the accident, the school bus driver has been released from his driving duties; according to Kinnicutt, his CDL has not been revoked, but he is no longer employed or driving a commercial vehicle.

During the police interview, the busdriver stated that he took medication daily for both a cardiac and a diabetic condition. He said that he had been taking this medication for about 12 years and believed that it had never affected his driving ability. He stated that he was feeling fine and was well-rested the morning of the accident.

The school bus driver's personal medical records indicated that the driver was receiving treatment for cardiac[13] and diabetic conditions as well as hypertension.[14] The

---

[9] His corrected vision was 30/40 in his right eye and 20/30 in his left eye, measured using a Snellen visual acuity test. In a statement to investigating police, the driver reported that he had been wearing his glasses while driving but could not locate them after the accident. Two chaperons stated that the driver was wearing his glasses while driving.

[10] New York Department of Motor Vehicles, *Commissioner Regulations*, Part 6, "Special Requirements for Busdrivers," require a biennial physical for all busdrivers.

[11] While exiting a school parking lot, the bus struck a road side sign, causing minor vehicle damage.

[12] Investigators contacted both the busdriver's daughter and police officers at his former office of employment but received no additional information on the driver.

[13] The busdriver had a heart attack in 1993 and experienced continuing symptoms of congestive heart failure and dyspnea (difficulty breathing). At that time, he was found to have a deep venous thrombosis and was prescribed the anticoagulant, coumadin, for this condition.

[14] The busdriver was prescribed atenolol to control his high blood pressure.

medical records noted that the driver did not follow prescribed dietary restrictions, did not routinely check his blood sugar, and on two occasions was "totally confused" about how much medication he was supposed to be taking for his diabetes.

The physician who conducted the busdriver's CDL physical examination on September 4, 1999, was not his personal physician and had access only to the medical history that the busdriver provided. The driver did not note treatment for congestive heart failure and did not list any of his cardiac medications or his anticoagulant.

The physician performing the CDL examination was aware that the driver was a diabetic, but did not direct the driver to obtain a 6-month reevaluation as required by the New York State Commissioner Regulations, Part 6, and the New York Department of Motor Vehicles (NYDMV), Article 19-A. Those requirements consist of "certification by the employee's personal physician that his or her condition has remained stabilized and that he or she has not had an incident of hypoglycemic shock since the last certification." No medical review of the busdriver's physical examination form was apparently performed by anyone, other than the examining physician. Kinnicutt also was aware of the busdriver's diabetic condition and requested a statement from his personal physician, to comply with the NYDMV regulations, regarding the driver's diabetic condition in November 1998. The driver's personal physician noted that "he has had no hypoglycemic attacks" but not whether the driver's condition was stabilized.

Truckdriver

The dump truckdriver held a valid, class B, New York CDL. The license had no endorsements and was only valid for intrastate operation. It was issued on September 5, 1997, and expires on October 16, 2002. A review of his driving record indicated that he was not involved in any other traffic accidents and did not have any citations.

School Bus Information

The school bus was manufactured in June 1997 by AmTran of Conway, Arkansas. AmTran rated the bus body to seat 66 children or 44 adults and to hold 13 standees. The bus had eight emergency exits: one side door and two window exits on the left side, two window exits on the right side, two roof hatches, and one rear door exit.

The bus chassis was manufactured by Navistar International Corporation in May 1997. The vehicle odometer at the time of the postaccident inspection read 44,291 miles.

The bus had been subject to two separate recalls by AmTran. The first recall was issued to replace the fuel supply lines on the engine. Corrective action was completed in August 1999. The second recall was issued for the flip seat by the side emergency exit door; the flip seat's hinge assembly had a potential for passenger injury[15] due to its

---

[15] Injuries caused by fingers and shoes being caught in the hinges.

scissoring action and its location near passengers. According to AmTran officials, the parts necessary to repair the hinge were sent to the bus operating company on September 7, 1999. The repairs were completed by HL Gage International on September 8, 1999.

The Safety Board performed a postaccident mechanical inspection of the school bus that included the power train, tire and wheel assemblies, brakes, steering, and suspension. The inspection revealed no vehicle operational defects or equipment deficiencies.

Damage

The Safety Board documented the impact damage to the school bus. The vehicle's fiberglass hood assembly was damaged and displaced at the forward hinge. The engine frame mounting and transmission bell housing were fractured, causing the engine and transmission to sag downward. The chassis' main frame rails were displaced to the left about 5.75 inches from their longitudinal axis. The bus body had 15 inches of intrusion on the right side behind the right rear axle. (See figure 1.) In addition to this contact damage, the bus had induced damage to side posts, roof bows, corner reinforcements, window frames and glass, the rear emergency exit door and frame, interior and exterior sheet metal and reinforcements, and the entrance door step well and frame area. The body-to-chassis mounting clips were found separated at the frame rail and at the floor panel deformation.

Side Emergency Exit Door

The side door had a release mechanism to allow occupants to open the door from the inside in the event of an emergency. (See figure 5.) The release mechanism consisted of a horizontal metal bar attached at one end with two bolted vertical locking rods. When in the locked position, the locking rods rest in apertures above and below the door. When the horizontal bar is pulled upward 90 degrees, the motion causes the two locking rods to move out of the apertures, and the door is released.

The horizontal bar extended 1.9 inches from the door surface. The bolts connecting the horizontal bar to the two locking rods extended 2.5 inches from the door surface. The door was also equipped with a metal support handle that was 8 inches wide and extended 4.5 inches from the door surface.

The Federal Motor Vehicle Safety Standards (FMVSSs)[16] prescribe the size of the door, the minimum spacing required for the aisle leading to the door, and the performance standards of the door release mechanism. The door release mechanism must allow manual release by a single person, from either inside or outside the vehicle. In addition, the interior opening mechanism must be operated in an upward motion, but the exterior mechanism's opening direction is at the discretion of the manufacturer. The mechanism can neither require the use of remote controls or tools nor be dependent on the vehicle's power supply.

---

[16] Title 49 *Code of Federal Regulations* Part 517.217.

Figure 5. View of side emergency door and "flip-up bottom" seat in the up position.

In this accident, a lap-belted chaperon (see 5C in figure 4) was in the flip-up bottom seat[17] adjacent to the side emergency exit door (see figure 5). Due to the dynamics of the collision, she was not initially propelled laterally into the door. However, the chaperon stated that after impacting the seat in front of her, she then fell toward the side emergency exit door. She sustained a left wrist strain and a thumb fracture.

Seat Cushion Bottoms

The school bus seat cushion bottoms were fixed to the seatframe with two hinges at the front and two latching clips at the base of the seat cushion bottom and seatback. (See figure 6.) After the accident, a number of these latching clips were found unlatched or loosely attached, so that the seat cushion bottoms were not fastened to the seatframes at the base of the bottom cushion and seatback. (See figure 7.) Some school buses are manufactured with seat attachments that are permanent, while others are manufactured with hinges and latches, such as on the accident bus. (The use of hinges and latches allows the removal or lifting of the seat cushion bottom for ease of cleaning.)

---

[17] Using this type of seat allows a seat to be placed adjacent to the side exit while maintaining the minimum width of 11.8 inches of aisle to the exit.

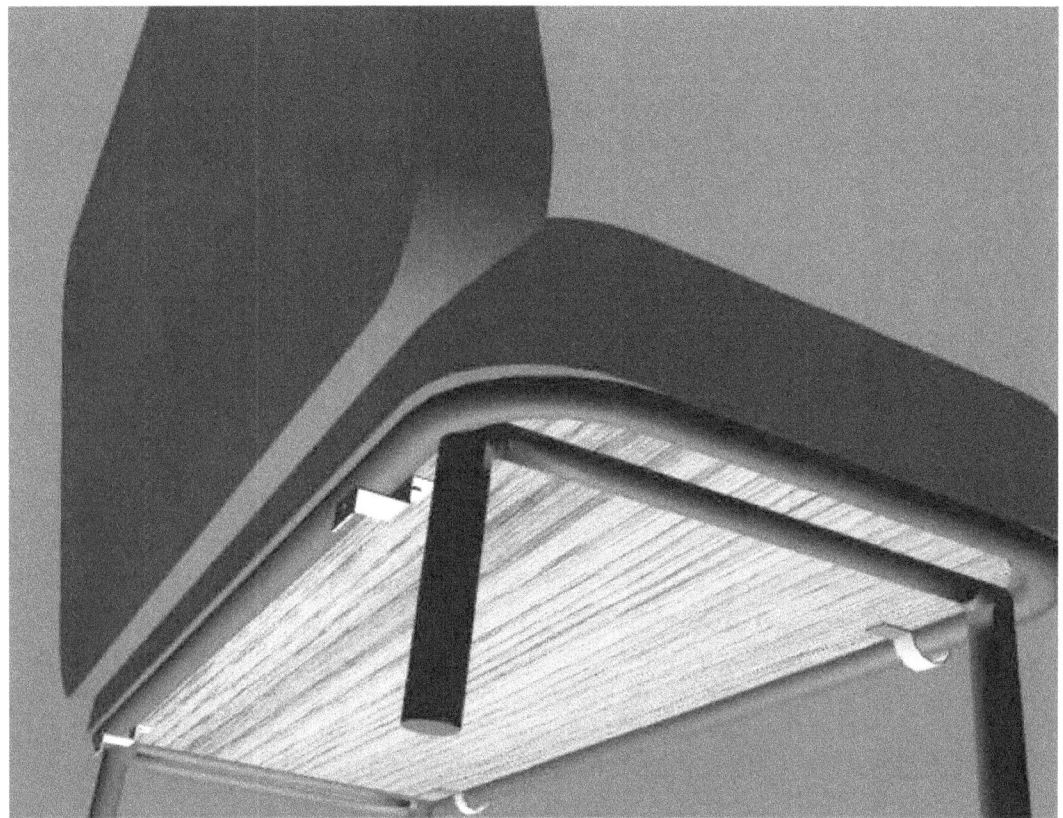

Figure 6. School bus seat cushion bottom, showing hinges and latching clips.

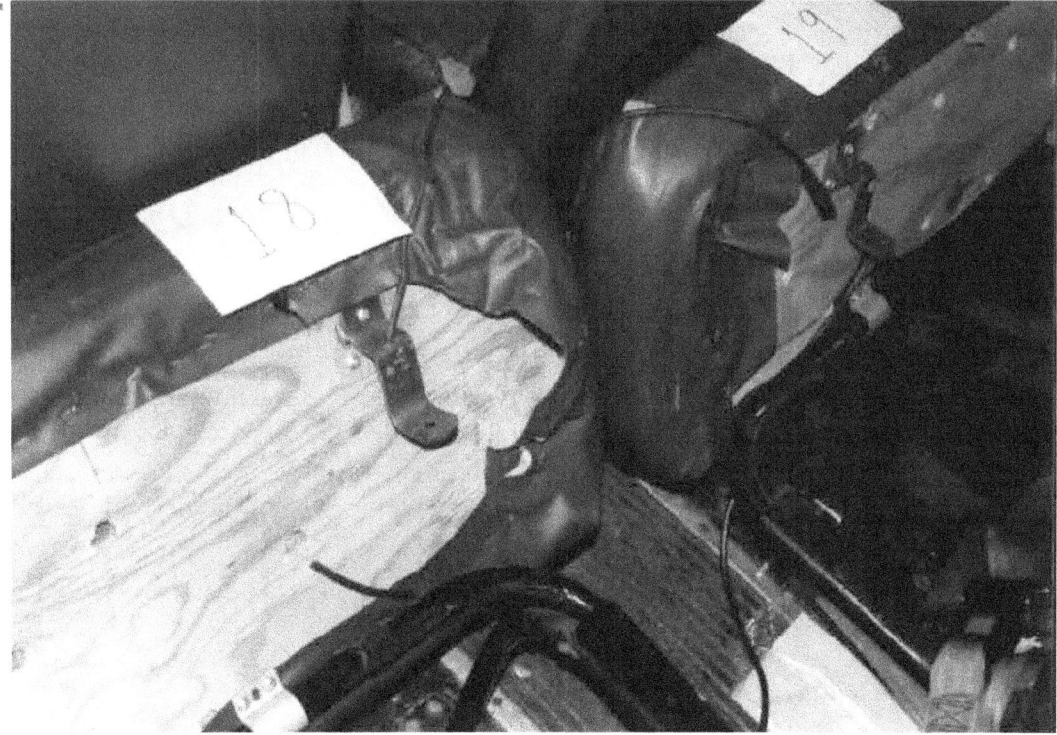

Figure 7. Postaccident view of the bottom of the seat cushions and latching clips.

The National Transportation Safety Board has issued several recommendations concerning the attachment of the bottom seat cushion to the seatframe. In 1984, a collision occurred between a school bus and tractor semitrailer in Rehoboth, Massachusetts.[18] During this collision, the school bus overturned and came to rest on its roof, causing many of the bottom seat cushions to become loose. As a result of this collision, the Safety Board asked that the National Highway Traffic Safety Administration (NHTSA):

<u>H-84-75</u>

For newly manufactured vehicles, revise *Federal Motor Vehicle Safety Standard Number 222* to include a requirement that school bus seat cushions be installed with fail-safe latching devices so as to ensure they remain in their installed position during impacts and rollovers.

In a December 23, 1985, letter, NHTSA responded that it had no evidence that the seat cushion securement mechanisms did not meet the requirements of FMVSS 222.[19] (The FMVSS states that the seat cushion must not separate from the seat at any attachment point when subjected to an upward force of five times the seat cushion weight.) The letter cited the example of a 1979 school bus that was included in compliance testing and passed FMVSS 222 requirements. Also, NHTSA stated that it determined the unlatching forces for seat cushion latching clips on a small sample of school buses. The resulting force failure thresholds were sufficiently high, relative to latching clip weights, to maintain the clip's attachment, even in a severe crash. It responded that, therefore, it did not believe that a revision or amendment to the standard could be justified at that time. NHTSA planned to notify school bus manufacturers and school bus operators through their associations and alert them to this problem.

In September 1986, NHTSA wrote to school bus manufacturers and operators alerting them to the potential problem of loose seat cushions. In 1987, NHTSA informed the Safety Board that three school bus manufacturers had replied that their new buses would have permanently attached seats. NHTSA then conducted a survey and found that the six largest manufacturers (80 percent of bus production) indicated that they would permanently affix the cushions in the future. Safety Recommendation H-84-75 was classified "Closed—Acceptable Alternate Action" on June 15, 1990.

In 1987, the Safety Board addressed the same issue in its safety study *Crashworthiness of Large Poststandard School Buses.*[20] During this study, the Board found that the bottom of seat cushions came loose in all types of school buses and accidents. The study stated that failure to refasten seat cushion bottoms after cleaning might pose safety hazards of causing additional injuries and hindering passenger

---

[18] National Transportation Safety Board. 1984. *Collision of G & D Auto Sales Inc. Tow Truck Towing Automobile, Branch Motor Express Company Tractor-Semitrailer, and Town of Rehoboth School Bus in Rehoboth, Massachusetts.* Highway Accident Report NTSB/HAR-84-05. Washington, DC.

[19] Title 49 *Code of Federal Regulations* 571.222.

[20] National Transportation Safety Board. 1987. *Crashworthiness of Large Poststandard School Buses.* Safety Study Report NTSB/SS-87/01. Washington, DC.

evacuation by allowing the seat cushion bottoms to loosen within the vehicle during a collision. As a result of the 1987 study, the Safety Board asked that the National Association of State Directors of Pupil Transportation Services (NASDPTS):

H-87-16

Advise school districts under your jurisdiction to emphasize to maintenance personnel that seat cushions must be securely reattached after removal and to remind school bus drivers to include seat cushion attachments as part of the pretrip inspection.

The New York director of pupil transportation responded to this recommendation that seat cushion securement would be addressed by the New York State Department of Transportation (NYSDOT) as part of its semiannual school bus vehicle inspection program. In addition, newsletters published by the New York Association for Pupil Transportation, the State education department, and the contractor association, would contain articles reminding mechanics and drivers of their responsibilities in this area. Between 1987 and 1995, Safety Recommendation H-87-16 was classified "Closed— Acceptable Action" for New York and 48 other States, plus the District of Columbia, and "Closed—No Longer Applicable" for Arkansas.[21]

Since the accident bus, manufactured in 1997, was equipped with the hinged and latched seat, buses are still being manufactured with this option. The Safety Board contacted school bus manufacturers and found that some are still using seat cushion bottoms that are not permanently attached to the seatframe. (See table 2.)

Table 2. School bus manufacturer information.

School Bus Manufacturer	Seat Cushion Bottom Attachment Used
American Transportation Corp.	Permanent and hinged
Blue Bird Corporation	Permanent
Carpenter Industries, Inc.	Hinged
Collins Bus Corporation	Permanent and hinged
Mid Bus, Inc.	Hinged
Thomas Built Buses	Hinged
Van-Con, Inc.	Permanent

---

[21] Arkansas has had a policy since 1985 requiring that school bus seat cushions be securely reattached after removal for maintenance.

Dump Truck and Trailer Information

The 1987 three-axle Mack Trucks, Inc., dump truck and the 1988 33-foot utility trailer were registered to and owned by MVF of Schoharie, New York. The vehicle combination weighed 32,650 pounds and had an overall length of 58 feet. The truck odometer reading at the time of the postaccident inspection was 187,049 miles.

Damage

The truck sustained a frontal impact, which caused major damage to the front fenders and engine cover, including headlight and signal assemblies. The hood radiator and battery boxes were also damaged. The windshield was broken on the driver's side. The postaccident wheelbase on the right side was measured at 202.5 inches and on the left side at 212.9 inches. The frame rails in the engine compartment had been deformed as much as 11.5 inches rightward.

Mechanical Condition

General and mechanical postaccident inspections of the dump truck disclosed a defect in the suspension system,[22] a defective brake light switch, and the lack of a tractor protection device. The Commercial Vehicle Safety Alliance (CVSA) lists these conditions as out-of-service violations in its *North American Standard Out-of-Service Criteria*.

The defective brake light switch resulted in a failure of the truck and trailer's rear brake lights. The utility trailer had a leaking air brake hose.[23] Although an air leak was found within the brake system, air loss rate testing indicated that even during a full brake application, the leak was insignificant and did not compromise the available air supply for braking. The dump truck was not originally manufactured to tow a trailer. Modifications were made to its air brake system to allow the trailer's brake system to be connected to the truck's system. No installed tractor protection device or system, commonly referred to as a tractor protection valve (TPV),[24] was found during the postaccident inspection. The TPV is designed to protect the towing vehicle's air supply during a trailer breakaway or when a severe air leak develops in either vehicle. Without a TPV, had the trailer had a catastrophic air leak, the tractor's air supply would not have been preserved and total brake failure would have occurred.

Tractor Protection Valve

The CVSA *North American Uniform Out-of-Service Inspection Criteria*; the *Federal Motor Carrier Safety Regulations, Minimum Periodic Inspection Standards*; the

---

[22] A spring-to-axle fastening device of the left third axle. One of the four axle clamp bolts was loose; no evidence of axle movement or shifting was found.

[23] The air hose was split near the forward left brake chamber.

[24] The valve is routinely used to control the trailer service and supply lines before disconnecting the trailer from the towing vehicle. The valve is typically near the rear of the towing vehicle and operates in conjunction with a dash-mounted control valve.

FMVSS 121 S5.1.3; and 49 *Code of Federal Regulations* (CFR) 393.43 address the requirement for a TPV on the accident truck.

Safety Board postaccident vehicle inspections revealed that the "glad hands"[25] on the rear of the accident truck had been plumbed into the existing air brake lines from the truck's third axle assembly. The trailer supply glad hand had been plumbed into the parking brake circuit of the third axle, and the trailer service glad hand had been plumbed into the service delivery line behind the third axle's relay valve. Both of the glad hands were additionally equipped with a manual shutoff valve. In this configuration and with the manual shutoff valves in the open position, an attached trailer was provided with an air supply source whenever the truck's parking brakes were released. Because the truck's parking brakes were held in the released position by air pressure, the trailer supply system was charged whenever the driver released the truck's parking brakes by supplying system air pressure to the parking brake circuit. In addition, because the trailer service line was plumbed directly into the truck's third axle relay valve delivery line, the trailer received a proportional air application signal whenever the truck's foot valve or hand-operated brake valve was activated.

The CVSA vehicle inspection procedures for the tractor protection valve and trailer bleed back inspections require that the inspector instruct the driver to release the vehicle emergency or parking brakes by pushing in the driver-accessible dash-mounted control valves and to exit the vehicle. Then, the inspector is to ask the driver to disconnect both air lines from the towing vehicle. After both lines have been disconnected, the inspector is to immediately check the trailer glad hands for escaping air. Although a brief and small amount of air discharge is normal, a steady or continual escape of air is indicative of a defective emergency relay valve on the trailer. When the air lines are disconnected, air begins to exhaust from the towing vehicle supply glad hand and may shut off quickly, around 60 to 70 pounds per square inch (psi). If air continues to escape below 20 psi of system air, the TPV is considered defective and an out-of-service condition exists.

When air stops exhausting from the supply line, the inspector is to ask the driver to return to the tractor and make a service brake application. If air exhausts from the service glad hand during the service brake application, the tractor protection valve is also considered defective and an out-of-service condition exists.

During their postaccident inspection, Safety Board investigators found that removing both the trailer air lines did not result in any unusual bleed back from the trailer emergency relay valve and that air ceased exhausting from the supply glad hand on the truck at 45 psi of system air. An additional inspection step revealed that upon a service brake application, the truck's remaining system air rapidly exhausted out of the service glad hand, indicating a defective TPV. Further inspection disclosed that the truck was not equipped with a TPV. If an inspector had not conducted the additional service brake

---

[25] The *Motor Truck Engineering Handbook,* fourth edition, defines a glad hand as "a separable mechanical connector used to join air line hoses when combination vehicles are coupled together."

application, the way in which the glad hands had been plumbed into the truck's original air system would have given a false indication that a TPV existed and was operating properly.

Vehicle Inspection

The MVF vehicles were subject to the New York vehicle inspection and maintenance regulations[26] requiring a minimum of one annual vehicle inspection conducted at an official inspection station that is licensed and registered with the NYDMV. Although the MVF has no maintenance records for the accident truck, it would have had to receive a minimum of 12 annual inspections to be registered in the State. The regulation inspection criteria[27] specifically require that a TPV be present and operating properly.

Additionally, under the Motor Carrier Safety Assistance Program, the MVF vehicles were subject to roadside inspections, which are conducted by the NYSDOT and the New York State Police. These roadside inspections employ the CVSA *North American Uniform Out-of-Service Criteria*, which require the presence and proper operation of a TPV on towing vehicles.

A carrier inspection profile, provided by the NYSDOT, indicated that between January 1988 and July 1998, three roadside inspections were conducted on the accident truck. Although some equipment violations were detected during these inspections, neither the roadside inspections, nor the 12 annual vehicle inspections, identified the absence of a TPV.

Highway Information

Intersection Description

SR-30A, at the south end of the intersection,[28] is a two-way, two-lane, paved asphalt roadway running north and south. The north- and southbound lanes are divided by a concrete median that is flush with the roadway. The northbound through-lane is 12 feet wide, and the southbound lane is 11 feet wide. Both are bordered by 11-foot-wide paved shoulders. At the northbound approach to the intersection, the roadway also consists of an 11-foot-wide left turn lane to accommodate traffic intending to proceed onto SR-7. (See figure 2.)

SR-7 is a two-way, two-lane, paved asphalt roadway running east and west through the intersection. At both approaches to the intersection, the roadway is divided by a concrete median that is flush with the roadway. The number of lanes at the intersection is increased by the addition of turn lanes. At the west approach of SR-7 is an 11-foot-wide

---

[26] *New York State Vehicle and Traffic Law*, Article 5, Part 79.

[27] Article 5, Part 79.27, "Heavy Vehicle Inspection."

[28] The roadway north of the intersection becomes Zicha Road.

westbound through-lane, a 4-foot-wide concrete median, a 10-foot-wide paved shoulder on the north side, and a 6-foot-wide paved shoulder on the south side. (See figure 2.)

The speed limit for both State routes is 55 mph.

Intersection Modifications

The NYSDOT had conducted several informal safety studies of the intersection between 1983 and 1993. These studies were initiated because of complaints made by members of the community concerning the overall safety of the intersection. In 1996, at the request of the State police, the NYSDOT conducted a formal highway safety investigation study[29] to determine the causal factors for an above-average number of motor vehicle crashes that had occurred at the intersection.

The NYSDOT highway safety investigation study reported that the intersection's sight distance exceeded the American Association of State Highway and Transportation Officials recommended guidelines[30] and that the flashing signal beacons were visible for a long distance in each direction. The pavement markings in the area of the intersection were rated good to poor. The centerline markings were observed to be in good condition; however, the stop lines were in poor condition.

The study also examined the intersection's accident history from January 1, 1992, through December 31, 1994. During that period, a total of 14 accidents[31] had occurred at or near the intersection. Of those 14 accidents, 11 were right angle collisions. All 11 of the accidents listed "Failure to Yield" as a contributing factor. Eighty-one percent of the drivers were more than 50 years old. Several accidents involved drivers who stopped for the stop sign and then pulled into the intersection into oncoming traffic.

A Safety Board review of the NYSDOT accident history records indicated that between January 1994 and June 1996, nine additional accidents occurred at the intersection. A total of 23 accidents took place from January 1992 until improvements were begun in June 1996.

According to the study, the total accident rate for intersection collisions at this location was 8.28 accidents per million vehicle miles, three times greater than the State average of 2.76 accidents per million vehicle miles. The intersection had a rate of 2.13 accidents per million entering vehicles, about five times greater than the State average of 0.38 accident per million entering vehicles.

On May 23, 1996, the NYSDOT made several recommendations to the Schoharie County resident engineer to modify the intersection's signing and pavement markings. In

---

[29] New York State Department of Transportation Report No. 955015.

[30] *A Policy on Geometric Design of Highways and Streets.* Chapter V: Local Roads and Streets. AASHTO. 1994. A roadway with a design speed of 50 mph should have a sight distance of 515 feet; at 60 mph the sight distance increases to 650 feet. This intersection had a sight distance in excess of 860 feet.

[31] One fatal, five injury, and eight property-damage-only accidents.

response to the recommendations, the intersection signing and pavement markings were modified between June 3, 1996, and June 4, 1997. (See table 3.)

Table 3. Modifications to intersection signing and pavement markings.

1. SR-7 westbound—replaced existing intersection sign with new intersection sign.
2. SR-7 eastbound—installed new intersection sign approximately 830 to 920 feet before intersection.
3. Zicha Road southbound—replaced existing "stop ahead" sign with new "stop ahead" sign.
4. SR-30A and Zicha Road approaches—removed old stop bars and installed new 24-inch stop bars about 5 feet from edge of pavement. Included painted word STOP on pavement. Placed additional double yellow barrier marking between new stop bar and color-contrasting median.
5. Intersection—installed roadside delineators[a] similar to example A in *Manual on Uniform Control Devices* figure 295-2.
6. SR-30A—checked nighttime reflectivity of existing stop sign and replaced sign.
7. Zicha Road—replaced existing stop sign with new stop sign.
8. SR-30A northbound and southbound—installed new "stop ahead" signs about 830 feet before intersection.

[a.]Road delineators are light-retroreflecting devices mounted in series at the side of the roadway to indicate the roadway alignment.

Following these modifications, the intersection's accident history was documented to determine whether the modifications succeeded in decreasing the accident rate at the intersection. (See table 4.)

Table 4. Intersection accident history after modifications.

Dates	Accidents
June through December 1996	5
January through December 1997	1
January through September 1998	3
November 1998 through March 1999	1

NYSDOT officials stated that they were satisfied with the reduction in accidents resulting from the 1996 intersection improvements. No further changes to the intersection or its related traffic control devices are planned. When questioned by Safety Board investigators about changing the intersection to a four-way stop configuration, NYSDOT officials responded that the NYSDOT had concluded that high-speed approaches to an intersection made the use of a four-way stop hazardous. In addition, the traffic volumes of the intersecting roadways differed significantly. Therefore, no such change would be made.

While conducting its 1996 study, the NYSDOT used the collected data to evaluate the need for conventional traffic signals at the intersection. Based on that data, NYSDOT officials determined that the intersection did not meet the *Manual on Uniform Traffic Control Devices* (MUTCD) warrants for traffic signals. After this accident, the Safety Board questioned the NYSDOT about the need for signals at this intersection. The NYSDOT initiated a formal study on November 15, 1999, to determine whether the intersection now met the MUTCD warrants for traffic signals. The results from this study found that the intersection still did not meet the MUTCD warrants; therefore, traffic signals were not installed.

Other Information

Requirements to Drive a School Bus

Federal Requirements. To drive a school bus, a driver must obtain a valid CDL, with a passenger endorsement, and a valid medical certificate.

New York Requirements for a Busdriver. The NYDMV, Article 19-A, imposes requirements applicable to all busdrivers licensed in New York. The State requires that the motor carrier file affidavits annually attesting to its compliance with the following requirements of Article 19-A for all busdrivers:

- A driver must be at least 18 years of age.

- A driver must not be disqualified to drive a motor vehicle.

- A background check[32] must be conducted on a driver.

- A driver's driving record for the previous 3 years must be obtained.

- A driver must be informed of the provisions of Article 19-A.

- A driver must have an initial physical examination and an examination biennially thereafter.

- A driver's driving record must be reviewed annually.

- A driver's defensive driving performance must be observed annually.

- A driver must perform a behind-the-wheel driving test biennially.

- A driver's knowledge of the rules of the road must be tested, either in writing or orally, biennially.

---

[32] Federal and State criminal and traffic.

New York Requirements for a School Bus Driver. In addition to those requirements for a busdriver, the State has additional requirements for a school bus driver, under the authority of the New York Department of Education, as follows:

- A driver must be at least 21 years of age.

- A driver must receive a physical exam annually.

- A driver must pass a physical performance test[33] biennially.

- A driver must receive at least 2 hours of instruction on school bus safety practices.

- A driver must receive 2 hours of refresher instructions in school bus safety biannually.

- A driver must provide three statements, pertaining to the driver's moral character and reliability, from people not related by blood or marriage.

Motor Carrier Requirements. In addition to the Federal and State requirements, Kinnicutt requires drivers to pass a Kinnicutt-administered road test before employment. After employment, the motor carrier requires drivers to take a written test on school bus operations and driving annually and requires the drivers' attendance at a defensive driving program biannually; the State only requires a written test to be administered biennially and requires drivers' attendance at a defensive driving program annually.

Medical Certification for Commercial Vehicle Drivers

Medical certification is required of all U.S. interstate commercial vehicle drivers who operate vehicles that weigh more than 10,000 pounds; carry 8 or more occupants, including the driver, for compensation; convey 15 or more occupants, including the driver, for no compensation; or transport hazardous materials requiring placards.[34]

A CDL applicant must be evaluated[35] and certified by a medical examiner and then be reevaluated biennially. The medical examiner may certify a driver for less than 2 years if the examiner believes that the driver's physical condition warrants monitoring.

A CDL applicant may visit any medical examiner who is licensed by, certified in, or registered with a State to perform physical examinations. Medical examiners may include doctors of medicine, osteopathy, and chiropractic; physician assistants; and advanced-practice nurses. Federal regulations require examiners to be familiar with the physical and mental demands facing commercial drivers. Instructions for performing and

---

[33] The physical performance test assesses a school bus driver's ability to perform the following functions: repeatedly open and close a manually operated bus entrance door, climb and descend bus steps, operate hand controls simultaneously and quickly, have a quick reaction time from the throttle to the brake, carry or drag individuals in a bus emergency evacuation, repeatedly depress the clutch or brake pedals, and quickly exit oneself and students through an emergency door.

[34] Title 49 *Code of Federal Regulations* 390.5.

[35] Title 49 *Code of Federal Regulations* 391.

recording physical examinations are available in these regulations.[36] Neither a Federal training nor a certification program is in place to ensure that examiners are familiar with the regulations. The Federal Motor Carrier Safety Administration distributes medical advisory criteria, upon request, and has maintained a Web site containing medical advisory criteria since 1997.

Although Federal regulations do not require the use of a standard medical examination form, they do specify and define the information that must be recorded. This information comprises the driver information and health history (which is completed by the applicant) and the physical evaluation and the medical certificate (which are effected by the medical examiner). Some States' forms do contain regulations and instructions for an examiner to use.

Federal regulations specify 13 conditions that should be evaluated during an examination, including impaired or lost limbs, cardiovascular impairments,[37] respiratory dysfunction, muscular impairments, diabetes, eyesight and hearing problems, mental disorders, and use of controlled substances. In general, a medical certificate is not to be granted to those with epilepsy, insulin-treated diabetes, and poor hearing or vision, as defined in the regulations. Other physical conditions may preclude an individual from obtaining a medical certificate,[38] and it is the responsibility of the examiner to determine whether the nature of the condition would present a potential hazard to the motoring public.

If a medical examiner believes that a driver is physically qualified to operate a commercial motor vehicle, the examiner is to complete the medical certificate and provide a copy to the driver and the driver's employer.[39] The driver must possess a copy of the certificate when driving; the motor carrier must maintain a copy of the certificate in the driver's qualification file.

Intrastate drivers are subject to their State regulations for physical qualification. New York has adopted legislation that is similar to the Federal requirements, with a few exceptions. For example, it requires elementary and secondary school bus drivers to have an annual medical examination. In addition, drivers with insulin-controlled diabetes are allowed to operate a commercial vehicle if their physicians have certified that they have not suffered hyperglycemic or hypoglycemic shock for 2 years and if they remain under adequate supervision and are recertified biannually. These recertifications must be maintained in the motor carrier's file, which is subject to inspection.

---

[36] Title 49 *Code of Federal Regulations* 391.43.

[37] Myocardial infarction, angina pectoris, coronary insufficiency, thrombosis, and hypertension.

[38] Title 49 *Code of Federal Regulations* 391.43.

[39] Title 49 *Code of Federal Regulations* 391.43(g) states, "If the medical examiner finds that the person he/she examined is physically qualified to drive a commercial motor vehicle in accordance with 391.41(b), he/she shall complete a certificate in the form prescribed in paragraph (g) of this section and furnish one copy to the person who was examined and one copy to the motor carrier that employs him/her."

Senior Drivers and Intersection Accidents

Accident statistics show that senior[40] drivers are overrepresented in intersection accidents.[41] For drivers 80 years and older, more than half of the fatal crashes occurred at intersections, compared with 24 percent for drivers under 50 years of age.[42] Most of these accidents involved a failure by the senior driver to yield the right-of-way.[43]

Several factors may account for the disproportionate number of intersection accidents involving senior drivers. These include limited head and neck movements,[44] slowed reactions to unexpected events, decreased visual acuity and contrast sensitivity, reduced ability to estimate the speed of approaching vehicles, and degradations in selective and divided attention.[45]

Studies show that older drivers generally exhibit declines in sensory, perceptual, and cognitive skills, although large individual differences exist in the rate of decline.[46] Early older-driver research focused on the relationship between visual-sensory degradations and accident involvement, but results suggested that degraded vision played only a minor role in accidents.[47]

More recent studies have focused on the attention and cognitive demands of driving. Research on "useful-field-of-view"[48] has shown that visual processing speed and the ability to handle selective and divided attention demands have a greater impact on accident rates. Although it was found that aging does not directly contribute to traffic accident involvement, aging was significantly correlated with lower processing speed and degraded attention.[49] Other research has found that older adults have more difficulty discriminating relevant from irrelevant information, especially during demanding search

---

[40] Usually considered to be 65 years and older.

[41] Staplin, L., Lococo, K., and Byington, S. *Older Driver Highway Design Handbook*. U.S. Department of Transportation. Federal Highway Administration. Publication No. FHWA-RD-135. 1998. Washington, D.C.

[42] *IIHS Facts. Elderly*. Insurance Institute for Highway Safety. 1993. July, Washington, D.C.

[43] *Transportation in an Aging Society: Improving Mobility and Safety for Older Persons*. Transportation Research Board. 1988. Washington, D.C.

[44] This reduces the driver's ability to scan the environment.

[45] Publication No. FHWA-RD-135. 1998. Washington, D.C.

[46] Sivak, M., Campbell, K.L., Schneider, L.W., Sprague, J.K., Streff, F.M., and Waller, P.F. "The safety and mobility of older drivers: What we know and promising research issues." *UMTRI Research Review*, 26(1). 1995.

[47] Ball, K., Owsley, C., Sloane, M., Roenker, D., Bruni, J. "Visual attentional problems as a predictor of vehicle accidents among older drivers." *Investigative Ophthalmology and Visual Science: Supplement 33*. 1993. and Schieber, F. "Effects of visual aging upon driving performance." *Proceedings of the Third International Symposium of Lighting for Aging Vision and Health*. 1995.

[48] Commonly used as a measure of selective attention, the useful field of view describes the amount of peripheral vision that an individual can attend to while performing a task located at the center of his or her visual field.

[49] Investigative Ophthalmology and Visual Science: Supplement 33. 1993. and Ball, K., and Rebok, G. "Evaluating the driving ability of older adults." *Journal of Applied Gerontology*, 13(1). 1994.

tasks.[50] In addition, older adults tended to respond more slowly to complex or unexpected events.[51]

NHTSA's Next Generation Safety Systems Research Plan

During the Safety Board's 1998 Bus Crashworthiness Public Hearing, NHTSA unveiled its Next Generation Safety Systems Research Plan, in which it intends to explore ways to enhance the interior safety environment for school bus occupants. The plan is now in its analysis stage. The research includes evaluating whether standards should be revised for occupant seating, restraints, and lateral surfaces, such as windows and sidewalls. Although not excluded from the research, the injury causing potential of side emergency exit doors is not specifically included in the research plan. As part of its research, NHTSA has performed full-scale crash testing on two school buses and is using the gathered data (acceleration-time histories) to perform sled tests using different restraint criteria and occupant sizes and seating conditions. NHTSA is evaluating the information obtained from these tests and expects to complete the report by spring 2001.

---

[50] Brouwer, W.H., Waterink, W., Van Wolffelaar, P.C., and Rothengatter, T. "Divided attention in experienced young and older drivers: lane tracking and visual analysis in a dynamic driving simulator." *Human Factors*, 33(5). 1991. and Ponds, R.W., Brouwer, W.H., and Van Wolffelaar, P.C. "Age differences in divided attention in a simulated driving task." *Journal of Gerontology*, 43. 1988.

[51] Vercruyssen, M., Carlton, B.L., and Diggles-Buckles, V. "Aging, reaction time, and stages of information processing." *Proceedings of the Human Factors Society 33rd Annual Meeting.* 1989.

Analysis

The accident in Central Bridge occurred because the school bus driver failed to stop the school bus before entering the intersection, even though he acknowledged afterward that he had seen the posted stop sign. Subsequently, the dump truck crashed into the right rear of the school bus, intruding 15 inches into the passenger compartment, which resulted in seven passengers sustaining serious injuries.

The major safety issues identified in this investigation are the potential for passenger injuries as a result of the school bus emergency exit door design and as a result of school bus seat cushion bottoms that are removable or hinged and the adequacy of commercial vehicle airbrake inspections.

After a discussion of factors that were considered and eliminated as causal or contributory to this accident, the analysis focuses on the major safety issues.

Exclusions

Highway Design

Due to the number of engineering improvements to and the accident history of the intersection, as well as the public concern about the safety of the intersection, the Safety Board investigated whether the design of the intersection could be causal in this accident. Between 1983 and 1997, the NYSDOT and Schoharie County completed a variety of engineering improvements to the accident intersection. These improvements were a byproduct of safety studies and a 1996 highway safety investigation conducted by the NYSDOT. Following these improvements, which included flashing control beacons, "stop ahead" signs, and pavement markings, the accident rate for the intersection declined from 5.1 per year between 1992 and 1996 to 3.6 per year between 1997 and 1999.

The NYSDOT, through its safety investigation and safety studies, concluded that the intersection sight distance was satisfactory and that the flashing control beacons were clearly visible. The NYSDOT also determined that a four-way stop was not appropriate for the intersection and that further modifications to the intersection and the traffic control devices were not necessary. Nevertheless, after this accident, the NYSDOT conducted a formal study to evaluate the need for conventional traffic signals at the intersection and determined that the intersection did not meet the MUTCD warrants for traffic signals.

The circumstances surrounding this accident suggest that the traffic control devices used to regulate the intersection did not contribute to the cause of the collision. Sufficient warnings existed at the intersection (an advance "stop ahead" warning sign, a stop sign, flashing beacons, and pavement markings) to alert a driver to stop. During a postcrash interview with police, the school bus driver stated, "I was looking for route 7. As I approached the intersection in front of me, I saw a stop sign on the right side of the road. I was so concerned trying to find route 7 that I didn't stop. I only slowed down. I didn't stop before crossing route 7." Not only were there multiple warnings for a vehicle to stop at the intersection, the busdriver acknowledged that he saw the stop sign yet he still continued through the intersection. The Safety Board concludes that sufficient traffic control warnings were provided at the intersection to alert drivers to stop.

Mechanical Condition of the Dump Truck

The postaccident mechanical examination of the dump truck and utility trailer revealed that the truck had a defective brake light switch, was missing a TPV, and had a loose bolt on the third axle spring-to-axle clamp. In addition, the utility trailer had a leaking air brake hose near the forward left brake chamber. The Safety Board examined these defects to determine whether they contributed or were causal to the accident.

The defective brake light switch caused the rear brake lights of the truck and trailer not to illuminate when braking occurred. Brake lights are intended to signal any following vehicles that the vehicle ahead is braking. Although this was an out-of-service condition and potentially dangerous in general, the defective brake light had no impact on this accident since no vehicle was behind the truck.

Suspension defects, such as the movement of a spring-to-axle clamp, can affect the dynamic response of a truck during heavy braking. However, no evidence was found to suggest that even though one of the axle bolts was loose, the axle or clamp moved. Therefore, the loose bolt was not a factor in the accident.

Although an air leak was found within the brake system, air loss rate testing conducted by the Safety Board indicated that even during a full brake application, the leak was insignificant and did not compromise the available air supply for braking. An analysis of the truck's braking was conducted to determine the vehicle's ability to produce adequate braking forces. In the accident load condition, the truck and utility trailer's braking efficiency was calculated to be between 99 and 100 percent. The braking efficiency analysis indicated that all brake assemblies were mechanically capable of producing adequate braking forces during the accident. The Safety Board concludes that although the dump truck and trailer had several mechanical defects, including a leaking air hose, those defects neither had an adverse effect on the vehicle's performance nor reduced the vehicle's braking capacity, and, therefore, the condition of the dump truck and trailer was not a factor in this accident.

School Bus Driver

The 79-year-old school bus driver stated that although he saw the stop sign at the intersection with SR-7, he did not stop because he was preoccupied with locating his destination. The Safety Board examined his actions to determine what conditions may have affected his driving performance.

Issues of selective attention may be particularly pertinent to this accident, given the circumstances before the accident and the age of the driver. This was the busdriver's first trip to the Pumpkin Patch, and chaperon statements suggest that the busdriver was confused as he searched for the correct exit off the interstate. The demands of finding an unfamiliar place, in the midst of passenger noise and activity, may have acted to narrow the driver's useful-field-of-view, contributing to his failure to perceive the oncoming truck. In addition, the driver stated that although he saw the stop sign, he was focused on reaching his destination. This suggests an inability to disengage his attention from his search task and may partly explain why the driver did not stop at the stop sign.

The busdriver's record before the accident did not suggest that he was experiencing any difficulties performing his job. However, passenger reports of the busdriver's confusion before the accident and his inability to attend to the critical driving task of stopping the bus at the intersection suggest that his selective attention may have been degraded due to the demands of the driving situation and factors associated with aging. Therefore, the Safety Board concludes that the busdriver's performance may have been affected by factors associated with aging.

The busdriver had multiple medical problems, which were not well controlled. The physician who conducted his CDL physical examination in September 1999 had access only to the medical history that was provided by the busdriver himself. The driver neither noted treatment for congestive heart failure nor listed any of his cardiac medications or his anticoagulant. The physician performing the examination was aware that the driver was a diabetic, but did not direct the driver to obtain a 6-month reevaluation as required by the New York State Commissioner Regulations and NYDMV. Apparently, no medical review of the driver's physical examination form was done by anyone, other than the examining physician.[52]

---

[52] The medical fitness of commercial drivers and the CDL medical examination will be analyzed in a forthcoming Safety Board special investigation report, which will include the circumstances of the Central Bridge accident. The issues to be discussed in the report include medical requirements for commercial drivers, adequacy of examiner training guidance and authority, drug testing and enforcement, and the sharing of driver information.

The special investigation was initiated due to the motorcoach accident that occurred in New Orleans, Louisiana, on May 9, 1999, in which 22 passengers died. The busdriver in the New Orleans accident had serious, preexisting medical conditions, including kidney failure and extremely poor heart function that resulted in congestive heart failure. The driver was being treated for these conditions while still operating a motor coach. In addition to these medical conditions, the busdriver's postaccident toxicology report found evidence of illegal drug use before the accident.

Kinnicutt was aware of the busdriver's diabetes and did request a statement from his personal physician about it in November 1998. This statement only partially fulfilled the State requirements for a 6-month diabetes followup. Those requirements "consist of certification by the employee's personal physician that his or her condition has remained stabilized and that he or she has not had an incident of hypoglycemic shock since the last certification." The driver's personal physician noted only that "he has had no hypoglycemic attacks" and did not note whether the driver's condition was stabilized. Kinnicutt did not technically fulfill the State requirements as the statement did not include an assessment regarding the stability of the busdriver's diabetic condition. Without this assessment, the driver should not have been eligible to drive. However, Kinnicutt did request and receive a medical statement regarding the driver's diabetes, and it is unreasonable to expect the company to be able to evaluate the physician's response at the level of detail required to note this subtle omission.

The driver's medical condition may have contributed to the accident in a number of ways. He could have been experiencing a significantly elevated blood sugar, which could have resulted in central nervous system effects that range from confusion to coma. Alternatively, he could have taken too much diabetes medication without eating and lowered his blood sugar, resulting in dizziness, confusion, or loss of consciousness. He could have had a mild heart attack and been suffering from congestive heart failure. He could have been experiencing difficulty breathing and, therefore, been distracted. He could also have had an abnormal heart rhythm, which could have resulted in a decreased blood supply to the brain. If the driver was even slightly dehydrated, the atenolol that he was taking for hypertension could have suppressed the normal heart rate increase to compensate for the dehydration, and he may have experienced dangerously low blood pressure. His blood may have been thinned more than necessary by his anticoagulant, increasing his risk of a minor hemorrhagic stroke. Each of these incidents could possibly have occurred, given his medical history.

The school bus driver indicated that he saw the stop sign at the intersection, yet failed to stop. Several chaperons stated that before the accident, the driver had appeared confused when he stopped on the exit 24 ramp. Both of these circumstances suggest that the driver may have been confused or impaired as he approached the intersection. The busdriver's focus away from the critical task of stopping the bus at the intersection may have been because of impairment due to one or more of his medical conditions. Therefore, the Safety Board concludes that the busdriver's performance may have been affected by his medical condition.

School Bus Occupant Crash Protection Systems

In September 1999, the Safety Board adopted the special investigation report *Bus Crashworthiness Issues*[53] that analyzed six school bus accidents involved in impacts with large vehicles. The investigation was initiated to determine whether restraints on school bus seats, as currently designed, would have better protected the occupants in these accidents. The report concluded that it could not be determined whether the current design of available restraint systems for large school buses would have reduced the risk of occupant injury in the six accidents.

As a result of the special investigation, the Safety Board recommended to NHTSA on November 2, 1999, that:

H-99-45

In 2 years, develop performance standards for school bus occupant protection systems that account for frontal impact collisions, side impact collisions, rear impact collisions, and rollovers.

H-99-46

Once pertinent standards have been developed for school bus occupant protection systems, require newly manufactured school buses to have an occupant crash protection system that meets the newly developed performance standards and retains passengers, including those in child safety restraint systems, within the seating compartment throughout the accident sequence for all accident scenarios.

In its March 3, 2000, letter to the Safety Board, NHTSA replied that it is currently working on a 2-year research program that will scientifically determine the real-world effectiveness of current Federal requirements for school bus occupant crash protection and will evaluate alternative occupant crash protection systems in controlled laboratory tests. The NHTSA school bus research program is due to be completed by mid-2001. Pending completion of the NHTSA research and the development of performance standards, the Safety Board classified Safety Recommendations H-00-45 and -46 "Open—Acceptable Response" on August 24, 2000. As a result its investigation of the Central Bridge accident, the Safety Board reiterates Safety Recommendations H-00-45 and -46 to NHTSA.

In the Central Bridge accident, the school bus was equipped with three lap belts per seat, and the chaperons reported that most of the students were wearing them during the impact. Thus, the Safety Board considered the effectiveness of lap belts for mitigating injuries. A general analysis of the probable kinematics of the bus occupants was performed, followed by computer simulation of the probable kinematics of occupants in two different locations within the bus: the area of maximum intrusion and the side emergency exit door.

---

[53] National Transportation Safety Board. 1999. *Bus Crashworthiness Issues*. Highway Special Investigation Report NTSB/SIR-99/04. Washington, DC.

Occupant Kinematics

During the initial accident sequence, the forward movement of the bus was stopped by the impact with the dump truck. This impact most likely caused the passengers on the right side of the bus, seated rearward of the bus's center of gravity, to be propelled to the right. These passengers may have struck window frames, glazing, and the sidewall. The passengers on the left side of the bus, seated rearward of the center of gravity, were also propelled toward the right side of the bus; however, they most likely hit the seatback in front, the edges of seats, and other passengers. The passengers seated forward of the center of gravity were most likely propelled forward and to the right as the bus slowed from the impact of the dump truck.

After the initial impact, the forward movement of the dump truck caused the bus to rotate clockwise about 145 degrees. During this movement, the passengers, if initially seated on the right side, most likely moved laterally toward the right side of the bus. The passengers, if initially seated on the left side, may have struck the sides of seats or other passengers. The passengers on the left side of the bus who were unrestrained may have slid laterally and out of the seating compartment, depending on their initial positions.

The available lap belts were not designed to limit upper body movement; thus, the upper bodies of those restrained passengers were free to pivot about the pelvis. Due to the passengers' age and stature, their lower extremities may have moved in the same manner as their unrestrained upper bodies. Those passengers who were unrestrained moved in the stated directions. Once the bus came to rest, the unrestrained passengers may have landed on the floor or in the aisle.

The vehicle dynamics were simulated[54] to determine the severity of the crash. The results obtained from the simulation indicate that the bus and the truck were traveling about 23 and 39 mph, respectively, at impact. As a result of the collision, the bus underwent a change in velocity of about 13 mph at the center of gravity, while also experiencing a rotation change in velocity of about 115 degrees per second. Because of this, the crash forces experienced by passengers at the rear of the bus were greater than those at the bus' center of gravity.

A biomechanical study[55] was conducted using the software program *Graphical Articulated Total Body*[56] to model occupant kinematics based on the severity of the crash and the developed crash forces. Two areas of the school bus were examined for this study. The first area was row 10 on the right side of the bus (see figure 4): the area of maximum intrusion and the location of the most severely injured occupants. Three passengers were seated in this row; one unrestrained chaperon was seated on the aisle side, and two 7-year-

---

[54] Using the Engineering Dynamics Corporation Simulation of Automobile Collisions (version four), a two-dimensional simulation analysis of vehicle collisions based on the "smac" model originally developed by Calspan for the National Highway Traffic Safety Administration. Version four has been expanded to allow multiple vehicles, trailers, or barriers to be analyzed.

[55] *Accident Reconstruction Study: Biomechanics*, National Transportation Safety Board Docket No. Highway-00-001.

[56] Developed by Collision Engineering Associates.

old lap-belted students were seated in the middle and on the window side. Restraint use effects and lap belt slack were examined for these occupants.

The second area of study was row 5 on the left side of the bus (see figure 4). This row was adjacent to the side emergency exit door and was occupied by a lap belt-restrained chaperon. Occupant kinematics were examined to determine whether contact between a simulated occupant and the unprotected surfaces of the side emergency exit door may have occurred during the collision.

Occupant Kinematics (Simulation): Row 10, Area of Impact

The first simulation placed two 7-year-old restrained passengers with an unrestrained adult.[57] The male chaperon reported that some slack remained in the students' lap belts; as a result, belt slack was examined for this seating condition. Three different belt slack amounts were looked at: 0 inch, 1 inch, and 2 inches.

The following trends were seen for each measure of belt slack, although the more slack present in the belts, the farther forward the two simulated restrained occupants traveled. The simulation results indicated that the simulated occupant closest to the window (seat 10F)[58] hit the adjacent window and sidewall. The simulated occupant in seat 10E traveled forward of the simulated occupant in seat 10F and then struck the window and sidewall. In addition, head and body contact occurred between these two simulated occupants. The simulated occupant in seat 10D traveled farther forward than the other two simulated occupants due to the lack of restraint use. This simulated occupant collided with the other two simulated occupants, resulting in the simulated occupant in seat 10E being pushed farther forward.

The predicted injury patterns from these simulations did not exactly match the actual injuries sustained by occupants, but trends were still evident. The differences are believed to be a result of the inability to simulate the damage to the bus window and sidewall in this region of the bus, which was the area of maximum intrusion. This is a current limitation of the simulation software.

The study then explored hypothetical cases in which all occupants were either unrestrained, restrained by lap belts, or restrained by lap/shoulder belts. In addition, the final scenario looked at the predicted injury levels if the simulated occupants in seats 10E and 10F were alone on the seat.

The results from the simulations indicated that the two simulated 7-year-old occupants were predicted to receive similar injury levels, either restrained by a lap belt or unrestrained, when seated adjacent to an adult chaperon. Further, the same occupants were predicted to receive similar injury levels for either restraint condition if seated alone.

---

[57] This seating arrangement and restraint use are believed to be representative of the conditions present at the time of the collision.

[58] See figure 4 for all seating references.

Occupant Kinematics (Simulation):
Row 5, Adjacent to Side Emergency Exit Door

The simulated occupant motion for the occupant in seat 5C, the seat adjacent to the side emergency exit door, was such that the occupant moved away from the side emergency exit door in both the unrestrained and lap belt-restrained conditions. In the unrestrained condition, the initial impact was with the adjacent seatback followed by motion into or towards the aisle, depending on the simulated occupant's initial seating position. Furthermore, the simulated occupant motion indicated that the simulated occupant moved away from the unprotected area during the rest of the collision sequence. In the restrained condition, the initial motion was again forward and lateral toward the right. Due to the action of the lap belt, the simulated occupant did not contact the seatback in front but hit the seat cushion as the upper body rotated about the fixed pelvis. The simulated occupant was predicted not to hit the side emergency exit door in any restraint condition.

Summary of Occupant Kinematics

Similar injury patterns were noted between restrained and unrestrained occupants throughout the bus away from the impact area. The principal differences noted in injury patterns were based on the occupant location within the bus, as opposed to restraint usage. Occupants in the area of impact were more seriously injured than those occupants seated away from the impact area. In this accident, both restrained and unrestrained occupants may have been cushioned laterally by other occupants in the same seating area, reducing overall lateral motion and possible injury. In the case of the two 7-year-old occupants seated in row 10, the simulation suggested that, either restrained or unrestrained, they would sustain less severe injuries if seated alone.

The Safety Board concludes that it could not be determined whether being restrained by the lap belts available to the occupants of the accident school bus reduced the risk of injury.

School Bus Side Emergency Exit Door

Federal regulations permit a seat to be positioned adjacent to a side emergency exit door if the seat cushion bottom automatically assumes a vertical position when not in use; therefore, a bus passenger may be seated directly against the side emergency exit door. The size and spacing, as well as door release mechanism performance standards, are prescribed in FMVSSs 49 CFR Part 571.217; however, the regulations do not contain design requirements for the release mechanism and associated hardware.

Although the side emergency exit door of the accident bus met Federal regulations, it presented a safety hazard for passengers. Components of the side emergency door release mechanism protruded from 1.9 to 4.5 inches into the occupant compartment adjacent to the seat. These components consisted of unprotected metal rods, bars, a handle, and bolts. None of these components were padded or recessed for occupant protection. If struck by an occupant seated beside the door during an accident sequence, these surfaces could easily result in minor to serious, and possibly lethal, blunt force injuries to that occupant.

In this accident, a restrained chaperon was in the flip-up seat adjacent to the side emergency exit door. Due to the dynamics of the collision, this passenger was not initially propelled laterally into the door. However, she stated that after hitting the seat in front of her, she then fell towards the side emergency exit door. Although the passenger did not first strike the door, handle, or locking rods, the potential for lateral motion into this door during a side impact situation existed. In the simulation, the unrestrained occupant hit the side of the seatback with a force equivalent to approximately 14 times her body weight. If the dump truck had hit the bus on the opposite side, this occupant would have struck the side emergency exit door and protruding structures with considerable force, sufficient to have caused significant, and possibly fatal, injuries. In addition, many of the other passengers may have received their injuries by moving laterally during the accident sequence and then striking the sidewalls and windows.

In the report *Bus Crashworthiness Issues,*[59] the Safety Board noted that some passengers not seated in the area of intrusion were seriously or fatally injured in school buses involved in lateral impacts with large vehicles. Some of these injuries were sustained when occupants struck the sidewalls. Of the six school buses that were examined during the special investigation, only one was equipped with a side emergency exit door. No occupants were seated adjacent to the door or in any of the seats surrounding the door.

The Safety Board concludes that the potential exists for injuries to school bus passengers seated adjacent to emergency exits with protruding door handles and latches during side impact or rollover accidents. Current FMVSSs do not address the protection of those passengers seated adjacent to emergency exits with protruding door handles and latches because the standards do not contain design requirements. Therefore, the Safety Board believes that NHTSA should modify the FMVSSs to prohibit protruding door handles or latching mechanisms on emergency exit doors. In addition, the Safety Board believes that the NASDPTS should inform its members of the potential for injury to child passengers from protruding door handles or latching mechanisms on emergency exit doors. Consider not placing children in those seat positions adjacent to emergency exit doors so equipped.

School Bus Seat Cushion Bottoms

During the accident, a number of the school bus seat cushion bottoms were displaced because the latching clips at the base of the seat cushions were unlatched or loosely attached. As a result, two lap belt-restrained passengers in row 10 on the right side

---

[59] Highway Special Investigation Report NTSB/SIR-99/04.

came to rest, still restrained, with their knees almost touching the bus floor and their backs against the seat cushion.

The occupant kinematics for these passengers seated in the impact area indicate that the forces during the collision caused the passengers to move toward the sidewall and forward as the bus rotated after the initial impact. During the accident sequence, their seats most likely flipped upward at the hinges (attached to the front frames) due to the lack of proper securement and the passengers' forward movement onto the front of the seat cushions.

Both of the seriously injured passengers' (row 10) lateral and forward movements during the accident sequence (and possibly belt slack) resulted in their slipping under their lap belts and coming to rest with their backs on the seat cushion and their knees near the floor. The lap belts, with the pivoting seat cushion, may have resulted in higher forces during the impact of the passengers' lower extremities with the seatback in front and the sidewall. The Safety Board concludes that the school bus passengers, whether lap belt-restrained or unrestrained, may have sustained more severe injuries because the seat cushion bottoms were unlatched.

Since 1984, the Safety Board has found seat cushion latching to be an issue in a number of investigations and has recommended solutions concerning the attachment of the bottom seat cushion to the seatframe. Most school bus manufacturers indicated in a 1987 NHTSA survey that they would permanently affix the seats in future production; however, the accident bus, manufactured in 1997, was equipped with the hinged and latched seat. The Safety Board also discovered that many school bus manufacturers are still using seat cushion bottoms that are not permanently attached to the seatframe. Furthermore, since a number of the seat cushion bottoms on the accident bus were found improperly secured during the postaccident inspection, the Safety Board is concerned that the inspection of the latches by the States or operators does not ensure that the seat cushion bottoms are securely reattached to the seatframe after routine cleaning. Therefore, the Safety Board believes that NHTSA should modify the FMVSSs to include the requirement that school bus seat cushion bottoms be installed with fail-safe latching devices to ensure they remain in their installed position during impacts and rollovers. Additionally, the Safety Board also believes that the NASDPTS should inform its members again of the safety hazards of not ensuring that the seat cushion bottom latching clips are properly latched at all times.

Dump Truck Airbrake System

Mechanical inspection of the dump truck airbrake system by Safety Board investigators revealed the absence of a tractor protection system. This system is required[60] to protect the air supply of the towing vehicle in case of a catastrophic failure in the trailer brake system.

---

[60] *Federal Motor Vehicle Safety Standards* 121 section 5.3.

This vehicle was originally manufactured as a chassis, and the dump truck body was later added to the chassis. The vehicle had been modified, by adding a hitch and altering the airbrake system, to make it capable of towing a trailer with an airbrake system. The Safety Board contacted the chassis manufacturer, the body manufacturer, and the owner to determine who modified the vehicle for towing. The owner claimed that the body manufacturer performed the modifications, but the body manufacturer had no records of performing the service and did not believe that it would have done so.

The CVSA vehicle inspection procedures for a tractor protection system require the inspectors to instruct the driver to release the vehicle's emergency or parking brakes, exit the vehicle, and then disconnect both air lines from the towing vehicle. After both lines are disconnected, the inspector is to check the trailer glad hands for escaping air. A second check is to occur when the air stops flowing from the supply line. The inspector must then ask the driver to return to the tractor and make a service brake application.

In the accident vehicle, Safety Board investigators found that removing both the trailer air lines did not result in any unusual bleed back from the trailer emergency relay valve and that air ceased exhausting from the supply glad hand on the truck at 45 psi of system air. Upon a service brake application, the truck's remaining system air rapidly exhausted out of the service glad hand, indicating a defective tractor protection system. Because of the manner in which the glad hands had been plumbed into the truck's original air system, failure to conduct the additional service brake application would have given a false indication that a TPV existed and was operating properly.

This vehicle underwent as many as 15 separate mechanical inspections in its lifetime, performed by different inspectors and agencies. A carrier inspection profile indicated that three roadside inspections were conducted between 1988 and 1998. The vehicle was operated for 12 years and over 187,000 miles without any inspector ever discovering the absence of a TPV. Because this equipment deficiency was never detected, the Safety Board concludes that when inspecting the tractor protection system, inspectors may have assumed during the first inspection step that the tractor protection system was present and working as required, so they did not perform the second step, which was applying the service brake. Therefore, the Safety Board believes that the Federal Motor Carrier Safety Administration, the Maintenance Council of the American Trucking Associations, and the CVSA should advise their staff or members of the importance of requiring a brake application during inspections of tractor protection systems and the consequences of not doing so, as evidenced by the circumstances of this accident.

Conclusions

Findings

1. Sufficient traffic control warnings were provided at the intersection to alert drivers to stop.

2. Although the dump truck and trailer had several mechanical defects, including a leaking air hose, those defects neither had an adverse effect on the vehicle's performance nor reduced the vehicle's braking capacity, and, therefore, the condition of the dump truck and trailer was not a factor in this accident.

3. The busdriver's performance may have been affected by factors associated with aging.

4. The busdriver's performance may have been affected by his medical condition.

5. It could not be determined whether being restrained by the lap belts available to the occupants of the accident school bus reduced the risk of injury.

6. The potential exists for injuries to school bus passengers seated adjacent to emergency exits with protruding door handles and latches during side impact or rollover accidents.

7. The school bus passengers, whether lap belt-restrained or unrestrained, may have sustained more severe injuries because the seat cushion bottoms were unlatched.

8. When inspecting the tractor protection system, inspectors may have assumed during the first inspection step that the tractor protection system was present and working as required, so they did not perform the second step, which was applying the service brake.

Probable Cause

The National Transportation Safety Board determines that the probable cause of this accident was the school bus driver's failure to stop for the stop sign due to his degraded performance or lapse of attention as a result of factors associated with aging or his medical condition or both.

Recommendations

As a result of its investigation, the National Transportation Safety Board makes the following recommendations:

To the National Highway Traffic Safety Administration:

Modify the *Federal Motor Vehicle Safety Standards* to prohibit protruding door handles or latching mechanisms on emergency exit doors. (H-00-28)

Modify the *Federal Motor Vehicle Safety Standards* to include the requirement that school bus seat cushion bottoms be installed with fail-safe latching devices to ensure they remain in their installed position during impacts and rollovers. (H-00-29)

To the Federal Motor Carrier Safety Administration:

Advise relevant staff of the importance of requiring a brake application during inspections of tractor protection systems and the consequences of not doing so, as evidenced by the circumstances of the October 21, 1999, accident in Central Bridge, New York. (H-00-30)

To the National Association of State Directors of Pupil Transportation Services:

Inform your members of the potential for injury to passengers from protruding door handles or latching mechanisms on emergency exit doors. Consider not placing passengers in those seat positions adjacent to emergency exit doors so equipped. (H-00-31)

Inform your members again of the safety hazards of not ensuring that the seat cushion bottom latching clips are properly latched at all times. (H-00-32)

To the Maintenance Council of the American Trucking Associations and the Commercial Vehicle Safety Alliance:

Advise your members of the importance of requiring a brake application during inspections of tractor protection systems and the consequences of not doing so, as evidenced by the circumstances of the October 21, 1999, accident in Central Bridge, New York. (H-00-33)

The National Transportation Safety Board also reiterates the following recommendations:

To the National Highway Traffic Safety Administration:

In 2 years, develop performance standards for school bus occupant protection systems that account for frontal impact collisions, side impact collisions, rear impact collisions, and rollovers. (H-99-45)

Once pertinent standards have been developed for school bus occupant protection systems, require newly manufactured school buses to have an occupant crash protection system that meets the newly developed performance standards and retains passengers, including those in child safety restraint systems, within the seating compartment throughout the accident sequence for all accident scenarios. (H-99-46)

BY THE NATIONAL TRANSPORTATION SAFETY BOARD

James E. Hall
Acting Chairman

John A. Hammerschmidt
Member

John J. Goglia
Member

George W. Black, Jr.
Member

Carol J. Carmody
Member

Adopted: November 14, 2000